SAN DIEGO CHARGERS

BY BRIAN HOWELL

The Child's World®

Published by The Child's World®
1980 Lookout Drive • Mankato, MN 56003-1705
800-599-READ • www.childsworld.com

Acknowledgments
The Child's World®: Mary Berendes, Publishing Director
Red Line Editorial: Editorial direction
The Design Lab: Design
Amnet: Production

Design Element: Dean Bertoncelj/Shutterstock Images
Photographs ©: Eric Bakke/AP Images, cover; Tom
Walko/Icon Sportswire, 5, 7; AP Images, 9; Ric Tapia/
Icon Sportswire, 11; Denis Poroy/AP Images, 13; Kent
Horner/AP Images, 14–15; Charles Baus/Icon Sportswire,
17; Alan Mothner/AP Images, 19; Orlando Ramirez/Icon
Sportswire, 21; Paul Spinelli/AP Images, 23; Juan Salas/
Icon Sportswire, 25; Kevin Terrell/AP Images, 27; Lenny
Ignelzi/AP Images, 29

ISBN 9781634070027
LCCN 2014959708

Printed in the United States of America
Mankato, MN
July, 2015
PA02265

ABOUT THE AUTHOR

Brian Howell is a freelance writer based in Denver, Colorado. He has been a sports journalist for nearly 20 years and has written dozens of books about sports and two about American history. A native of Colorado, he lives with his wife and four children in his home state.

TABLE OF CONTENTS

GO, CHARGERS!

The San Diego Chargers started in Los Angeles, California. But they did not stay there for long. They moved south after one year to their current home. The Chargers have a gold lightning-bolt logo. They have not won a **Super Bowl**. But they are often in the hunt for the **playoffs**. San Diego has had many **Hall of Fame** players. Let's meet the Chargers.

Tight end Antonio Gates scores a touchdown in a game against the Seattle Seahawks on September 14, 2014.

WHO ARE THE CHARGERS?

The San Diego Chargers play in the National Football **League** (NFL). They are one of the 32 teams in the NFL. The NFL includes the American Football Conference (AFC) and the National Football Conference (NFC). The winner of the AFC plays the winner of the NFC in the Super Bowl. The Chargers play in the West Division of the AFC. They played in the Super Bowl after the 1994 season.

Running back Ryan Mathews (24) led the Chargers in rushing yards each year from 2011 to 2013.

WHERE THEY CAME FROM

A new professional football league started in 1960. It was called the American Football League (AFL). The Los Angeles Chargers were one of its first teams. The team was named in a fan contest. Los Angeles already had the NFL's Rams. So the Chargers moved to San Diego in 1961. They played in the AFL Championship Game five times from 1960 to 1965. They won the title after the 1963 season. The AFL ended after the 1969 season. So the Chargers joined the NFL.

Running back Keith Lincoln (22) tries to avoid a tackle in an October 7, 1962, game against the Dallas Texans.

WHO THEY PLAY

The San Diego Chargers play 16 games each season. With so few games, each one is important. Every year, the Chargers play two games against each of the other three teams in their division. Those teams are the Denver Broncos, Kansas City Chiefs, and Oakland Raiders. The Chargers also play six other teams from the AFC and four from the NFC. The Chargers have been **rivals** with the other AFC West teams since 1960. They all played in the AFL's West Division.

San Diego has been battling the Oakland Raiders for more than 50 years.

WHERE THEY PLAY

The Chargers played in the Los Angeles Memorial Coliseum in 1960. Then they left for San Diego. They played in Balboa Stadium from 1961 to 1966. In 1967, the Chargers moved to San Diego Stadium. It is now called Qualcomm Stadium. It is still their home. The Chargers share it with the San Diego State University football team. The San Diego Padres baseball team played there from 1969 to 2003. The stadium held 52,000 fans at first. Now it holds more than 71,000.

Fans love to get together outside Qualcomm Stadium before Chargers games.

THE FOOTBALL FIELD

END ZONE

HASH MARKS

BENCH AREA

14

MIDFIELD

SIDELINE

GOAL POST

20-YARD LINE

GOAL LINE

END LINE

BIG DAYS

The Chargers have had some great moments in their history. Here are three of the greatest:

1963—It was time to celebrate. The 1963 Chargers won the AFL Championship. They beat the Boston Patriots 51-10 on January 5, 1964. Running back Keith Lincoln led the way. He had 329 total yards and two **touchdowns**.

1994—The 1994 Chargers went 11-5 in the regular season. Then they made it to the Super Bowl on January 29, 1995. They lost 49-26 to the San Francisco 49ers. But fans loved seeing their team in the big game.

LaDainian Tomlinson put together one of the best seasons ever by a running back in 2006.

2006—San Diego won a team-record 14 games. The Chargers scored almost 31 points per game. That led the NFL. Running back LaDainian Tomlinson was the league's Most Valuable Player (MVP).

TOUGH DAYS

Football is a hard game. Even the best teams have rough games and seasons. Here are some of the toughest times in Chargers history:

1978—It was September 10. The Chargers led the Oakland Raiders 20-14. There were ten seconds left. Raiders quarterback Ken Stabler fumbled forward on purpose. Another Raider kicked the ball. Oakland recovered it in the end zone. They won by one point. The game is known as "The Holy Roller" game. The NFL later changed rules to stop such plays from happening.

2000—The Chargers went 1-15. They almost lost all their games. But kicker John Carney saved them on November 26. His **field goal** late in the fourth quarter gave them a 17-16 win over the Kansas City Chiefs.

The Chargers had a painful 2000 season.

2006—Quarterback Philip Rivers took over as starter. The Chargers went 14-2. They had high hopes for the playoffs. San Diego met the New England Patriots on January 14, 2007. The Chargers allowed 11 points in the final five minutes to lose 24-21.

MEET THE FANS

The Chargers have loyal fans. They love the team no matter what. The Chargers missed the playoffs from 1966 to 1978. But they finally made it back in 1979. Jerry Marcellino and David Sieff were two very happy fans. They worked in the music business. They wrote the "San Diego Super Chargers" disco song. It was performed by Captain Q. B. and the Big Boys. The song is still popular with Chargers fans.

Chargers fans love getting loud to support their team on game days.

HEROES THEN

Wide receiver Lance Alworth was a superstar. He led the AFL in receptions, receiving yards, and touchdowns three times each. Quarterback Dan Fouts played from 1973 to 1987. He led the NFL in passing yards four times. Running back LaDainian Tomlinson was great from 2001 to 2009. He rushed for 1,815 yards and 28 touchdowns in 2006. Linebacker Junior Seau was a strong defender. He was the team's Defensive Player of the Year twice.

Quarterback Dan Fouts was inducted into the Pro Football Hall of Fame in 1993.

HEROES NOW

Quarterback Philip Rivers is the team leader. He started every game from 2006 to 2014. Rivers passed for at least 4,000 yards in five of those seasons. Tight end Antonio Gates played college basketball. He uses his jumping skills to make great catches. Gates is among the best offensive tight ends of all time. Safety Eric Weddle was an All-Pro from 2010 to 2013.

Quarterback Philip Rivers made six Pro Bowls from 2006 to 2014.

GEARING UP

NFL players wear team uniforms. They wear helmets and pads to keep them safe. Cleats help them make quick moves and run fast. Some players wear extra gear for protection.

THE FOOTBALL

NFL footballs are made of leather. Under the leather is a lining that fills with air to give the ball its shape. The leather has bumps or "pebbles." These help players grip the ball. Laces help players control their throws. Footballs are also called "pigskins" because some of the first balls were made from pig bladders. Today they are made of leather from cows.

Defensive back Eric Weddle is one of San Diego's defensive leaders.

FACE SHIELD

HELMET

SHOULDER PADS

THIGH PADS

FOOTBALL

CLEATS

SPORTS STATS

ere are some of the all-time career records for the San Diego Chargers. All the stats are through the 2014 season:

PASSING YARDS
Dan Fouts 43,040
Philip Rivers 36,665

RUSHING YARDS
LaDainian Tomlinson 12,490
Paul Lowe 4,972

INTERCEPTIONS
Gill Byrd 42
Dick Harris 29

TOTAL TOUCHDOWNS
LaDainian Tomlinson 153
Antonio Gates 99

SACKS
Leslie O'Neal 105.5
Shaun Phillips 69.5

POINTS
John Carney 1,076
LaDainian Tomlinson 918

Wide receiver Charlie Joiner played with the Chargers from 1976 to 1986.

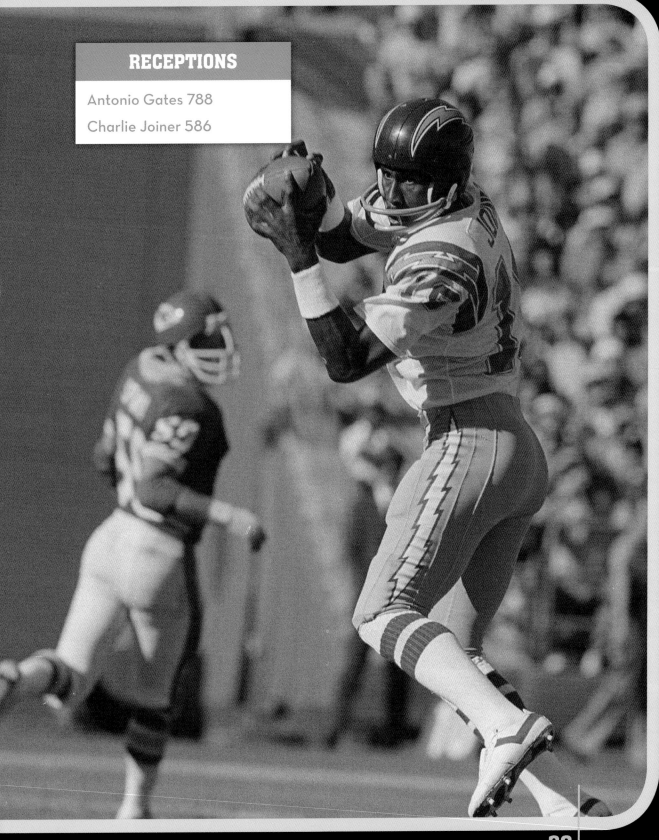

GLOSSARY

field goal a method of scoring worth three points in which a player kicks the ball between the goal posts

Hall of Fame a museum in Canton, Ohio, that honors the best players

league an organization of sports teams that compete against each other

Most Valuable Player (MVP) a yearly award given to the top player in the NFL

playoffs a series of games after the regular season that decides which two teams play in the Super Bowl

rivals teams whose games bring out the greatest emotion between the players and the fans on both sides

Super Bowl the championship game of the NFL, played between the winners of the AFC and the NFC

touchdowns a play in which the ball is held in the other team's end zone, resulting in six points

FIND OUT MORE

IN THE LIBRARY

Brooks, Sid, and Gerri Brooks. *Tales From the San Diego Chargers Sideline: A Collection of the Greatest Chargers Stories Ever Told.* New York: Sports Publishing, 2014.

Editors of Sports Illustrated Kids. *Football: Then to WOW.* New York: Time Home Entertainment, 2014.

Whiting, Jim. *The Story of the San Diego Chargers.* Mankato, MN: Creative Education, 2014.

ON THE WEB

Visit our Web site for links about the San Diego Chargers:
childsworld.com/links

Note to Parents, Teachers, and Librarians: We routinely verify our Web links to make sure they are safe and active sites. So encourage your readers to check them out!

INDEX